PRESIDENTIAL CONVENTIONS

PRESIDENTIAL CONVENTIONS

CHRISTOPHER HENRY

A FIRST BOOK

FRANKLIN WATTS
A Division of Grolier Publishing
New York London Hong Kong Sydney
Danbury, Connecticut

For General James P. Cullen, Esq.—
whose brilliant wit, endless generosity, and unfailing loyalty have
enriched the lives of so many of his compatriots.

With friendship and respect.

Cover photographs copyright ©: The Bettmann Archive; UPI/Bettmann (inset).

Photographs copyright ©: UPI/Bettmann: pp. 8, 34, 41, 45, 55; Reuters/Bettmann: pp. 17, 28; The Bettmann Archive: pp. 24, 27, 49, 57; AP/Wide World Photos: pp. 11, 19, 39, 42; The Gamma Liaison Network; pp. 13 (Joe Traver), 15 (Dirck Halstead), 37; The Library of Congress: pp. 20, 23, 47; North Wind Picture Archives: pp. 31, 52; Archive Photos: p. 33.

Author photograph copyright ©: Jane Jesse Cardinale

Library of Congress Cataloging-in-Publication Data

Henry, Christopher.
    Presidential conventions / Christopher Henry.
        p. cm. — (A First book)
    Includes bibliographical references and index.
    Summary: Traces the process of nominating both parties' presidential candidates, from the primary elections to the conventions where the choices are finally made.
    ISBN 0–531–20219–4
    1. Presidents—United States—Nomination—Juvenile literature. 2. Political conventions—United States— Juvenile literature. [1. Presidents—Nomination. 2. Politics, Practical.]   I. Title. II. Series.
    JK521.H47 1996   95–45288
    324.6'3'0973—dc20   CIP
                                                                  AC

CONTENTS

PRESIDENTIAL CONVENTIONS

The floor of a presidential convention is a sea of colorful campaign posters and state signs around which delegates gather.

ONE

National Conventions in the Television Age

Every four years, during the late summer, Americans tune in to a pair of events that are part political theater, part press conference, and part carnival. They are the national conventions of the Democratic and Republican parties. To understand them is to understand much about U.S. politics.

Political parties in the United States have held national conventions to select presidential candidates since the 1830s. In many ways, national party conventions have changed little from the first conventions. The main tasks of past and present conventions remain the same: to nominate presidential and vice presidential candidates, to unite the party behind a common set of political beliefs and goals, and to make the rules that govern the party and its members.

In other ways, conventions have changed greatly over the years. Reforms in election laws and party policies allow a greater diversity of Americans to become a part of the conventions. The method of choosing **delegates**—the party members who represent each state at the convention—has changed radically. And the events themselves have grown much bigger. In 1860, 466 Republican delegates chose Abraham Lincoln as their presidential **nominee.** In 1988, 2,277 Republicans gathered to nominate George Bush. But perhaps the greatest changes in the national political conventions can be explained by the role of television in the proceedings.

The first television coverage of the conventions was broadcast in 1952. Today an estimated 150 million viewers watch the events on national television. Television has gradually come to dominate the conventions. Viewers at home can see more of news anchors and reporters on the convention floor than of the presidential and vice presidential nominees. The

Television and electronic technology, such as these large projection screens used at the 1992 Republican convention, have taken on increasing importance at presidential conventions.

parties, in turn, recognize the importance of reaching the huge audience of television viewers and tailor their conventions to prime-time television.

All in all, the result is an emphasis on the public aspects of conventions: speeches, celebrity appearances, and visual spectacles. Hundreds of thousands of dollars are invested in banners and streamers, balloons and confetti, stages and orchestra pits, and projection screens and electronic gadgetry. Less emphasized are the deal making and internal party business that have always been part of conventions.

Before the era of television, conventions were less predictable and less planned. Often, nominees were not selected until after party leaders had met at the convention and worked out compromises. Delegates sometimes had to vote again and again until they could agree on a single candidate. In 1880, for example, Republicans had to take a vote, or **ballot**, thirty-six times before they settled on James Garfield—a record for Republican conventions.

Since 1952, however, no party has taken more than a single ballot to choose a presidential nominee. In fact, the parties' nominees are usually known well in advance of the conventions. Conventions, then, have become a valuable opportunity to present candidates to a national audience of potential supporters,

Television and radio newspeople roam the
convention floor, seeking out the latest story.
Delegates take time to talk with these reporters
and promote their party's candidates.

and party leaders work hard to avoid any appearance
of conflict or disorder at the conventions.

At televised conventions, party leaders also work
hard to build enthusiasm and excitement. The idea is
to show a nation of future voters that the party
faithful are energetically behind the candidate. The
wild applause that goes on and on whenever a speaker
predicts victory, the upbeat music, and the colorful

banners all work to build momentum for the candidate. At the 1992 Democratic national convention, party leaders chose a song by the rock group Fleetwood Mac to symbolize the youthful energy of candidates Bill Clinton and Al Gore.

Conventions usually do build support for candidates, at least for a while. Convention coverage failed to increase the popularity of only one candidate: Democrat George McGovern in 1972.

Planning for the conventions is extensive. Virtually every detail seems orchestrated to provide maximum effect. Even the site of the convention can help deliver a political message. The city of the convention site is usually selected more than a year before the event. The parties look for locations with a large convention hall or arena, a good transportation system, and plenty of hotel rooms for thousands of delegates, party leaders, reporters, and visitors.

They also look for sites with symbolic significance. In 1980, the Republicans chose to meet in Detroit, Michigan, a city with a strong labor union, to convey a desire to welcome labor unions into the party. In 1988, the Republicans held their convention in New Orleans, Louisiana, to emphasize the growing importance of southern voters to the party.

Despite all the drama associated with national

Young supporters of George Bush wave flags and signs at the 1992 Republican convention, which took place in Houston, Texas.

conventions, much of the actual business that takes place at the conventions can be unexciting. The proceedings usually last for four days. For both parties, the agenda begins with welcoming speeches and opening ceremonies, and then passes on through a series of reports from various committees and party officials during the first two days.

The highlight of the first day is the **keynote address**, sometimes made by an up-and-coming star in the party. The keynote can help launch a politician's national career, as it did for Bill Clinton in 1988. Then a young governor from Arkansas, Clinton gave a speech remembered more for its prolonged length than its content, but the occasion put him in the national spotlight.

On the second day, the platform committee reports. A party **platform** is the statement of policies and political views adopted by a party or candidate. Although it does not necessarily reflect the views of the party nominee, the party platform does reflect the current thinking of the party. Various groups in each party do a great deal of bargaining before they reach an agreement on a platform. The committee report reveals the results of those negotiations.

Only on the third day do delegates get around to presidential nominations and balloting. When convention delegates are divided between several nominees, the event can be suspenseful and exciting. The 1976 Republican convention battle between Gerald R. Ford and Ronald Reagan, for example, went down to the wire, with Ford winning on the first ballot with

In 1992, Mario Cuomo, then governor of New York, took the stage to nominate Bill Clinton for president at the Democratic convention.

just over 52 percent of the delegate votes. More often, the party's choice for nominee is clear before going into the convention. Nevertheless, delegates take the opportunity to speak about the qualifications of their candidates and supporters demonstrate, marching around the convention floor cheering, chanting, and waving their signs.

Once all nominations are made, balloting begins. Although the voting is usually just a formality, the event is the most famous of all convention traditions. The convention's secretary takes a roll call of the delegations state by state, in alphabetical order. The chair of each state's delegation announces his or her delegation's vote. A candidate needs a majority of all votes to win the party's nomination.

On the fourth day, the vice presidential nominee is chosen. Although nominations for vice president are made and a roll call taken, this procedure is simply a formality. According to custom, the presidential nominee is permitted to chose his or her running mate.

The convention concludes with the acceptance speeches of the presidential and vice presidential nominees. The two appear on stage together for the first time at the convention. If all has gone well for the party, the excitement generated by the conven-

On the last day of a convention, party nominees for president and vice president join hands and wave to the cheering crowds. Al Gore and Bill Clinton were the Democratic nominees in 1992.

tion spectacle will carry over and sustain the nominees through a successful campaign in the **general election** all the way to the White House.

When George Washington took the oath of
office as the first U.S. president in 1789,
political parties in the young country were
not firmly established.

TWO

The
Development
of American
Political Parties

America's founders could not have imagined national nominating conventions like the ones we have today. Nowhere in the U.S. Constitution are conventions even mentioned. Conventions evolved as part of the American political landscape.

The founders also did not plan for the two-party system to dominate American politics to the extent that it has. In fact, it was the emergence of strong national political parties in the early 1800s that created the need for conventions.

The first presidential election was uneventful. When George Washington was elected president in

1789 and 1792, he faced no significant opposition and won with a majority of electoral votes. The system back then, as stated in the Constitution, granted each state a number of **electors** that equaled the total of that state's representatives in both houses of Congress. Those electors met every four years to choose a president. Until the Constitution was modified in 1804, the candidate with the most electoral votes became president and the candidate with the second highest number of electoral votes became the vice president.

The Twelfth Amendment to the Constitution, passed in 1804, set up a new method of selecting the president and vice president. From that time forward, candidates would be elected separately by the **electoral college**, a body of electors chosen by voters from each state. This change in the Constitution enabled candidates for president and vice president to run as members of a team, or **ticket**, and to campaign together.

In the early days of American history, it was not uncommon for several candidates or tickets from the same political party to run against one another in the presidential elections. In 1824, for example, four major candidates from what was known as the Democratic-Republican party sought the nation's highest office. By the end of the Civil War, however, mem-

Originally the leader of the Jeffersonian Republicans, Thomas Jefferson is known as founder of the Democratic party.

bers of the various political parties had learned that it made more sense to settle differences among themselves, at national party conventions.

For over a century, American politics has been dominated by the Republican and Democratic parties. America's first two presidents, George Washington and John Adams, were members of another party—the Federalist party—which supported a strong federal government. The Jeffersonian Republicans, led by Thomas Jefferson, opposed the Federalists. Jefferson and his supporters, who came to be known as Democratic-Republicans, believed that the national govern-

After his 1828 win, Andrew Jackson, standing
on carriage seat, journeyed to Washington, D.C.
Along the way, crowds congratulated the
new president.

ment should have fewer powers and that states should have more say in conducting their own affairs.

After Federalist influence faded, the Democratic-Republicans dominated national politics from 1800 to 1824. Disagreements within the party caused a split: the Democrats led by Andrew Jackson and the National Republicans led by John Quincy Adams. In 1828, Adams lost to Jackson, who went on to a second term in 1832. The National Republicans, moderate supporters of a strong federal government and a stable national economy, fielded one more candidate for president—Henry Clay in 1832—and the party's short life was over.

A few years later, former National Republicans and others joined to form the Whig party. This party, a **coalition** of diverse elements, was difficult to categorize. Their common ground was an extreme dislike and distrust of Andrew Jackson and his followers. The Whigs won the White House in 1840 and 1848 but dissolved after the election of 1852.

The modern Republican party, which has survived as one of two major parties, was founded in 1854. The source of its strength and popular appeal lay in the party's opposition to slavery. Descended from several earlier antislavery parties, the Republican party was made up of many former Whigs and a substantial number of antislavery Democrats. In 1861, Abraham Lincoln became the first Republican president.

Since 1852, every president has been either a Democrat or a Republican. Out of the thirty-six elections held from 1852 to 1992, Republican candidates have won twenty-one times and Democratic candidates have been victorious fifteen times. Smaller parties and several independent candidates, however, have played an important role in American politics and some have exerted enormous national influence.

One of history's most notable third parties grew out of the Progressive movement, a campaign for social and political reform around the turn of the twentieth century. Progressives fought against the powerful and corrupt in business and government. Several Progressive candidates ran for president in several different elections, including former Republican president Theodore Roosevelt, who lost to Democrat Woodrow Wilson in 1912.

In 1924, Robert La Follette ran for the White House as a Progressive. He earned 16 percent of the popular vote and carried his home state of Wisconsin. In 1948, when Henry Wallace received only about 2 percent of the vote, the Progressive influence on American politics ended.

The first Republican president was Abraham Lincoln, who was inaugurated in 1861.

In 1992, billionaire H. Ross Perot ran for president as an
independent candidate.

In the 1948 election, another third-party candidate, Strom Thurmond of South Carolina, did not get
many more votes than Wallace. However, because his
influence was concentrated in the deep South, he
managed to carry four states and win thirty-nine electoral votes. Running under the States' Rights party
banner, Thurmond paved the way for other southern
candidates opposed to racial integration and federal
civil-rights legislation.

Alabama governor George Wallace ran for president as an independent candidate in 1968. Almost 10 million people voted for Wallace, who carried five southern states and won forty-six electoral votes. In 1992, H. Ross Perot, a wealthy businessman who had never held political office, declared his intention to run for president. Perot received more than 19 million votes, about 19 percent of the national total. Perot did not carry a single state, but his popular-vote total proved that it was possible for an independent or third-party candidate to be elected president.

Although the line between the two major parties has blurred somewhat in recent decades, differences still exist. One fundamental difference between the parties involves the federal government's role in running the country and spending its budget. Democrats tend to support a larger, more powerful central government than Republicans, who favor more powerful local governments. For example, for social programs, Democrats support administering funds through the national government while Republicans prefer giving block grants to local governments.

It is important to remember that while presidential candidates typically support their parties' platforms, any party member can and frequently does hold views that differ from official party positions.

THREE

From
Party Bosses
to
Superdelegates

When Americans vote, they choose from the candidates whose names appear on the ballot. Although **write-in votes** are permitted in most elections, very few people in the nation's history have ever been elected to office by a write-in vote. Out of the many hundreds who have served in the U.S. Senate, only one person was ever selected by a write-in vote: Strom Thurmond of South Carolina, in 1954. So American voters have a choice of leaders, but that choice is effectively limited to the candidates who

In a general election, the ballot lists just one presidential and vice presidential nominee from each party. The way parties choose these nominees has changed over time.

appear on the ballot. An important concern, then, is how these presidential candidates come to be placed on the ballot.

Historically, America's political parties have not

chosen their presidential and vice presidential nominees democratically. Until recently, ordinary Democratic and Republican party members had little influence—and no direct say—in the selection of the delegates who voted for their party's nominee at the national convention.

In the Republican and Democratic parties of the past, most delegates were appointed by members of Congress, governors, or other party officials. These influential party leaders, or **party bosses**, selected the delegates from among party loyalists. All too often, delegates—appointed by and accountable to the party bosses—voted as they were told to vote. The nominating process rested firmly in the hands of the party bosses and was far from democratic.

Delegates who rebelled and voted as they saw fit were not welcome at future party gatherings. Women, African-Americans, Latinos, poor people, young people—most Americans, in fact—did not share in party power or in political decision making. Their opportunity to voice opinions came only on general election day when they voted for either the Democratic or Republican nominee, or for an independent or third-party candidate whose chances of being elected were slim.

Political power, then, was concentrated in what

In the past, political power, including the selection of presidential nominees, rested with a small group of politicians and party insiders.

came to be known as the "smoke-filled rooms" of party bosses. The phrase refers to the deal-making sessions that the cigar-smoking party leaders engaged in at the party conventions. Even if the bosses had already agreed on a presidential candidate, there was still a great deal of business to conduct at the convention. The political spoils, which would be made available if the party's nominee won the presidency, included cab-

In 1984, Walter Mondale of Minnesota balanced the Democratic ticket with New York's Geraldine Ferraro. She became the first female vice presidential nominee for a major party.

inet positions, federal judgeships, multimillion-dollar public works projects, defense contracts and military installations, ambassadorships, and thousands of high-paying government jobs.

Also up for negotiation was the selection of the vice presidential nominee. The U.S. Constitution prohibits members of the electoral college from voting for a president and vice president who are both from the same state as the elector. Because of this restriction, political parties have always nominated presidential and vice presidential candidates from different states.

"Balancing the ticket" is not just a product of this constitutional law; it is also believed to improve a party's chance of winning the presidency. Parties frequently balance their tickets by pairing candidates from two different regions to appeal to the regional and state pride of voters in various parts of the country.

Unbalanced tickets have occurred in the past and won. In 1992, the Democrats fielded two southerners from neighboring states: Bill Clinton of Arkansas for president and Al Gore of Tennessee for vice president.

For nearly two centuries the smoke-filled room was a center of power in American politics, and to some extent, it still is. Making deals and trading votes for favors remains very much a part of politics. What has changed significantly is the diversity of the participants. No longer are women and members of racial, religious, and ethnic minorities shut out of the political process.

Starting in the 1960s, both parties began to make substantial reforms in the delegate selection process. The majority of delegates are now elected democratically. Most of the elected delegates are pledged delegates, delegates who have sworn to support a particular candidate for president.

The Democratic party rules also allow for a substantial number of "unpledged" and unelected delegates, called **superdelegates**. These superdelegates are members of Congress or hold other high elected offices or positions of prominence in the party. The Republican party rules specifically state that "there shall be no automatic delegates to the national convention who serve by virtue of party position or elective office."

Unpledged delegates are free to vote for the candidates of their choice. Pledged delegates, however, are free to vote as they please only if the candidate to whom they are pledged withdraws before or during the national convention, or if the convention has not been able to decide on a nominee after a number of ballots have been taken.

Although a firmly entrenched policy of discrimination existed for more than a century of presidential conventions, women and minorities now attend conventions as delegates.

In 1964 and 1968, the Democratic national convention adopted resolutions intended to prohibit discrimination based on "race, sex, age, color, creed, national origin, religion, ethnic identity, sexual orientation, economic status, philosophical persuasion or physical disability." The Democrats also adopted a broad plan for the delegate selection process that called for "specific goals and timetables for African-Americans, Hispanics, Native Americans, Asian-Pacific Americans, and women" and for equal division "as far as mathematically practicable" of delegate seats between males and females.

By the 1960s black voters in the South over-whelmingly supported the Democratic party. The Democrats had done much to win black support since the 1940s, including championing a number of civil-rights laws. Still, Democratic party state organizations in the South remained almost entirely segregated. Black voters often provided more votes than did southern whites, who were increasingly drawn to the Republican party. Few African-American delegates, however, were part of convention activity.

At the Democratic national convention of 1968, which is remembered for conflicts over civil rights and America's involvement in the war in Vietnam, the party's resolutions and plans for diversity were tested. The test involved Georgia governor Lester Maddox, who was elected on a promise to fight all forms of racial integration.

At the time, some states held **primary elections**, which allowed voters some choice in the selection of delegates to the presidential convention. In the state

Lester Maddox tried to derail the Democratic party's commitment to racial diversity at its 1968 convention, but his efforts failed.

of Georgia, there were no primary elections. Governor Maddox chose most of the state's 106 delegates to the convention, and like Maddox, most of those delegates were white.

Democratic party rules, however, insisted that the racial composition of state delegations be about the same as the state's Democratic voters. The Georgia Democratic Party Forum, a group of Democrats opposed to Governor Maddox, challenged the Maddox delegation. They asked the convention's credentials committee to seat their delegation instead, because it had been chosen at an open convention and was racially balanced.

After long debate, the credentials committee announced a compromise: both delegations would be seated with each delegate casting one-half of a vote instead of the usual full vote. Lester Maddox and his hand-picked delegation were furious. Shoving and punching members of the press, they stormed off the convention floor, taking the last remnants of the old Democratic party of the Confederacy with them. Never again would a segregationist play an important role at a Democratic convention.

Another high point of the 1968 convention came when Julian Bond, a twenty-eight-year-old black state senator from Georgia and leader of the newly seated Georgia delegation, was nominated for the vice presidential spot on the national ticket. Bond graciously declined because he was too young. (The Constitution requires that vice presidents be at least thirty-five years old.) Progress, however, had been made in the fight against discrimination.

These days, Democratic party rules provide for the

At the 1968 Democratic convention, Julian Bond
became the first African-American to be nominated
as vice president.

democratic election of most delegates through either
a primary election—an election in which voters of
each party select candidates to run for office—or a

In the primary election, party members from the general public vote for their party's presidential nominee.

caucus. A caucus is a meeting of a state's party members to choose that state's delegation to the presidential convention. In primary elections, all that is required of a voter is a brief appearance at the polls to cast a vote. Caucuses, however, are often daylong events, or a series of events, often held far from a voter's home. While primary elections often attract a large voter turnout, caucuses tend to be attended and dominated by very dedicated party activists.

The Republican party allows far greater leeway to the state organization in the selection of delegates than does the Democratic party. It permits the election of delegates by primary elections or party conventions and in some cases by the state Republican committee.

The Republican party has worked against discrimination in its system. Party rules declare that "each state shall take positive action to achieve the broadest possible participation by men and women, young people, minority and heritage groups, senior citizens, and all other citizens in the delegate selection process." They also specify that each state "shall endeavor to have equal representation of men and women in its delegation to the Republican National Convention."

FOUR

Convention History

During the first fifty years of the existence of the United States, political parties were controlled almost entirely by the party bosses. Candidates for president and vice president were nominated by congressional caucuses—where senators and representatives chose their parties' nominees—or endorsed by state legislatures. The failure of the parties to nominate candidates through a single, accepted procedure often resulted in several candidates claiming to be the nominee of a particular party.

At first, some states refused to participate in the

After party-boss control was loosened, presidential conventions became contentious, and many ballots were often required for delegates to agree on a nominee.

national conventions, but by the 1840s, it was generally accepted that the parties would choose their nominees only at these national meetings held every four years. If they were not yet democratic in their delegate selection procedures, the conventions' nomination processes were becoming truly democratic. No longer were all nominees named by a unanimous delegation on the first ballot. Instead, prolonged balloting over a period of days was frequently necessary to agree on a nominee.

In the late 1840s and 1850s, the national conventions became more than just meetings to select a party's nominees. They began to evolve into historically significant forums on social issues, like the existence and expansion of slavery. The candidate selection process grew ever more clumsy; in 1852, the Democrats and Whigs cast more than one hundred ballots between them to select their nominees. The national debate over slavery became so intense that it gave birth to its own political organization—the Republican party.

The first Republican to seek the presidency was John C. Frémont in 1856. Four years later, another Republican, Abraham Lincoln, won the White House. The value of the national convention's nominating process became readily apparent to Republicans in the midst of the Civil War.

In 1856, John C. Frémont became the first Republican to seek the presidency. Four years later, Abraham Lincoln became the first Republican to win it.

In 1864, President Lincoln sought a second term in office, despite strong resistance from some members of his own party and from antiwar Democrats. Many Democrats, however, supported the war effort, and it was with them that Lincoln's supporters within the Republican party forged an unusual coalition known as the "National Union" ticket. Lincoln accepted as his running mate Democrat Andrew Johnson, the governor of Tennessee. The National Union ticket was the only Republican-Democrat coalition ticket in the history of the United States. Interestingly, it led to a Democratic presidency less than a year later, when Lincoln was assassinated.

In 1912, the significance of primary elections, which a few states had begun holding by then, became clear to leaders from both parties. That was the year former president Theodore Roosevelt once again sought the Republican nomination for the nation's highest office. Roosevelt was exceptionally popular and was victorious in almost every primary election. However, the majority of Republican delegates was still chosen by the political bosses, and Roosevelt was denied the nomination.

Instead of meekly bowing out of the race, Roosevelt founded his own party and ran as an independent, winning more votes than the Republican candidate and ensuring victory for his Democratic opponent. Two facts were driven home to politicians: first, the people's choice is the best choice; second, party loyalty is not absolute, especially when the ordinary voter is shut out of the nominating process.

Since the mid-1800s, the Democratic party required that in order to win the nomination a candidate receive a two-thirds majority vote at the convention. By 1924, the dangers of the two-thirds rule were completely clear. That year, delegates to the Democratic national convention cast 103 ballots over a period of nine days before they chose a nominee, John W. Davis,

Although Republican party members voted for Theodore Roosevelt in the 1912 primary elections, he was denied the nomination and ran as a third-party candidate.

who was defeated in the November election by a land-slide. Today, both the Democrats and Republicans require only a simple majority of the delegates' votes to select a nominee.

FIVE

Pep Rally or Historic Meeting?

Many Americans have called upon the two major parties to institute a more democratic selection process for choosing presidential and vice presidential nominees. They propose dramatic changes that they say will give the voters a greater voice in the election of their leaders. Suggestions include scrapping the system of presidential conventions altogether and replacing it with a nationwide election or series of elections. These elections would allow party members to choose the nominees directly and limit the power of influential party leaders.

Although the American political convention has changed
with the times, its purpose remains the same: to
nominate party candidates for president and
vice president.

The direct election of nominees, however, would be difficult and risky. In practice, such a system could be disastrous. Without the expertise of party leaders and the flexibility needed to reach compromises, a party could find itself committed to a candidate with no chance of winning the general election.

The lengthy, grueling, and expensive primary process, which includes party meetings, caucuses, and elections, beginning almost a year before the national convention, weeds out the weakest candidates. Were it not for this process, all of these candidates could arrive at the convention, each with a tiny percentage of the national vote.

Scandals with the potential to damage a candidate's chances of election can also arise during a presidential primary campaign. Many candidacies have been destroyed by such disclosures in recent years. Democrat Gary Hart of Colorado had to withdraw from the 1988 race because of allegations of an extramarital affair. Allowing delegates to choose the nominees at the convention permits a party to rid itself of a candidate whose reputation has been harmed beyond repair.

However, at both Democratic and Republican conventions, nominees typically have their nominations firmly locked up weeks before the first delegates arrive at the convention halls. Several factors have contributed to this trend. Primary elections help narrow down the number of contenders for the nomination. Television coverage of the proceedings has also made the conventions more visible than ever, and party leaders labor hard behind the scenes to show the nation a united party at work on the convention floor.

Sometimes, the parties go so far that they stifle free speech, not only in the convention halls, but also on the surrounding streets. The most shocking example came in the summer of 1968, at the Democratic national convention in Chicago. Thousands of young demonstrators came to Chicago to protest U.S. involvement in the war in Vietnam. Democratic mayor Richard J. Daley of Chicago vowed that they would not be allowed to disrupt the convention.

While the convention went on, Chicago police attacked the mostly law-abiding and unarmed demonstrators. Hundreds of helmeted policemen charged into the crowds, beating young men and women bloody with billy clubs and fists. Hundreds were seriously injured; hundreds more were unlawfully arrested and jailed without cause. Some convention delegates and members of the press were also attacked. The television cameras captured all of it and millions

During the 1968 Democratic convention in Chicago,
police used rifle butts, tear gas, and clubs to battle the
antiwar demonstrators. The violence, shown on
television, shocked America.

of horrified Americans watched. The Democratic party's 1992 convention, in contrast, was notable for its almost complete lack of dissent and debate.

Whether full of discord or unity, today's conventions are hugely important to the two parties. Republicans and Democrats alike make the most of the opportunity to air free advertising to the nation's television audience. Critics call conventions nothing more than four-day-long pep rallies. Advocates call them historic meetings to inspire support for candidates and party platforms. Although the convention system may not be the most efficient or democratic way to choose presidential nominees, it has lasted in some form for more than 150 years and is not likely to disappear any time soon.

Presidential conventions, complete with colorful confetti and balloons, are familiar spectacles apt to continue their run for many more years.

GLOSSARY

Ballot—the piece of paper a voter uses to cast a vote; a round of voting

Caucus—a meeting of a state's party members to choose that state's delegation to the presidential convention

Coalition—a temporary union of political parties or organizations

Delegate—a party member who represents a state at the national convention

Elector—one of several representatives chosen by the voters of each state to elect the president and vice president

Electoral college—the body of electors chosen by voters from each state to elect the president and vice president

General election—the nationwide election in which the president and vice president are chosen

Keynote address—the speech given at national party conventions that is meant to address issues important to the party and to generate enthusiasm for the party platform

Nominee—the candidate chosen by a party to run for office

Party boss—a powerful party leader

Platform—the statement of policies and political views adopted by a party or candidate

Primary election—an election, held before the general election, in which voters select their party's candidates for office

Superdelegate—an unelected delegate, usually an important party member or a member of Congress, who is free to vote for the candidate of his or her choice. Only the Democratic party has superdelegates.

Ticket—a team of candidates nominated by a political party

Write-in vote—a vote cast for a candidate not listed on the ballot

FOR FURTHER READING

Blassingame, Wyatt. *The Look-It-Up Book of Presidents.* New York: Random House, 1990.

Feinberg, Barbara Silberdick. *Words in the News: A Student's Dictionary of American Government and Politics.* New York: Franklin Watts, 1993.

Hanneman, Tamara. *Election Book: People Pick a President.* New York: Scholastic, 1992.

Harvey, Miles. *Presidential Elections.* Chicago: Childrens Press, 1995.

Pious, Richard M. *The Presidency.* Englewood Cliffs, N.J.: Silver Burdett Press, 1991.

Raber, Thomas R. *Election Night.* Minneapolis: Lerner Publications, 1988.

———. *Presidential Campaign.* Minneapolis: Lerner Publications, 1988.

Samuels, Cythnia K. *It's a Free Country! A Young Person's Guide to Politics and Elections.* New York: Atheneum, 1988.

Sullivan, George. *Campaigns and Elections.* Morristown, N.J.: Silver Burdett Press, 1991.

———. *Choosing the Candidates.* Morristown, N.J.: Silver Burdett Press, 1991.

INDEX

61

ABOUT THE AUTHOR

CHRISTOPHER HENRY is a New York attorney in private practice. He has written several books for children, including *Ruth Bader Ginsburg* and *Sandra Day O'Connor* for Franklin Watts. Mr. Henry is the author of two other First Books about the American political process: *Presidential Elections* and *The Electoral College*.